World of Music

Africa

Andrew Solway

Heinemann
LIBRARY

www.heinemann.co.uk/library

Visit our website to find out more information about **Heinemann Library** books.

To order:

☎ Phone 44 (0)1865 888066

🖹 Send a fax to 44 (0)1865 314091

💻 Visit the Heinemann Bookshop at www.heinemann.co.uk/library to browse our catalogue and order online.

First published in Great Britain by Heinemann Library, Halley Court, Jordan Hill, Oxford OX2 8EJ, part of Harcourt Education. Heinemann is a registered trademark of Harcourt Education Ltd.

Editorial: Louise Galpine, Harriet Milles,
          and Rachel Howells
Design: Victoria Bevan and Philippa Baile
Illustrations: Jeff Edwards
Picture Research: Hannah Taylor and Fiona Orbell
Production: Julie Carter

Originated by Chroma Graphics (Overseas) Pte. Ltd
Printed and bound in China

ISBN 978 0 4311 1777 5
12 11 10 09 08
10 9 8 7 6 5 4 3 2 1

British Library Cataloguing in Publication Data
Solway, Andrew
Africa. – (World of Music)
780.9'6
A full catalogue record for this book is available from the British Library.

Acknowledgements

The publishers would like to thank the following for permission to reproduce photographs: africanpictures.net pp. **10** (Independent Contributors/Cedric Nunn), **13** (South Photographs/Graeme Williams); Alamy Images pp. **18** (Jacques Jangoux), **38** (Eddie Gerald); ArenaPAL pp. **5**, **20**, **25**, **39** (Jak Kilby); Corbis pp. **8** (Michael Ochs Archives), **14** (Peter Johnson), **16** (PAP/Barbara Ostrowska), **32** (Charles O'Rear), **33** (Wendy Stone); Getty Images/Spencer Platt p. **26**; John Warburton-Lee pp. **22–23**, **30**, **31** (Nigel Pavitt); National Geographic Image Collection p. **19** (Michael Lewis); Panos pp. **12** (Giacomo Pirozzi), **17** (Matias Costa), **29** (Jacob Silberberg); Putumayo Records p. **9**; Redferns pp. **7** (Brigitte Engl), **11** (Peter Pakvis), **15** (Philip Ryalls), **27** (Jan Persson), **35** (Jon Lusk), **37** (Leon Morris), **40**, **42–43** (Philip Ryalls), **41** (Phil Dent); Reuters/Mike Hutchings p. **21**; Rex Features p. **34** (Oksanen); Still Pictures pp. **6** (Frans Lemmens), **24** (Henning Christoph).

Cover photograph of musician playing drum in Morocco, reproduced by Photolibrary/Workbook, Inc.

The publishers would like to thank Patrick Allen for his assistance in the preparation of this book.

Contents

Welcome to African music   4

African instruments   10

Putting on the style   16

Rhythm and song   22

Everyday music   28

Modern African music   34

Growing and changing   42

A world of music   44

Glossary   46

Further information   47

Index   48

Some words will be printed in bold, **like this.** You can find out what they mean by looking in the glossary.

Welcome to African music

You may have heard African music at home or on the radio. Even if you haven't, you probably know something about the music of Africa without being aware of it. There are African sounds and **rhythms** in almost every kind of popular music. **Blues**, jazz, rock, Latin music, **reggae**, **soul**, rap, **hip hop**, and many other styles have connections with African music. To find out why these connections exist, we have to look at the history of Africa. But before we do, let's explore the African continent.

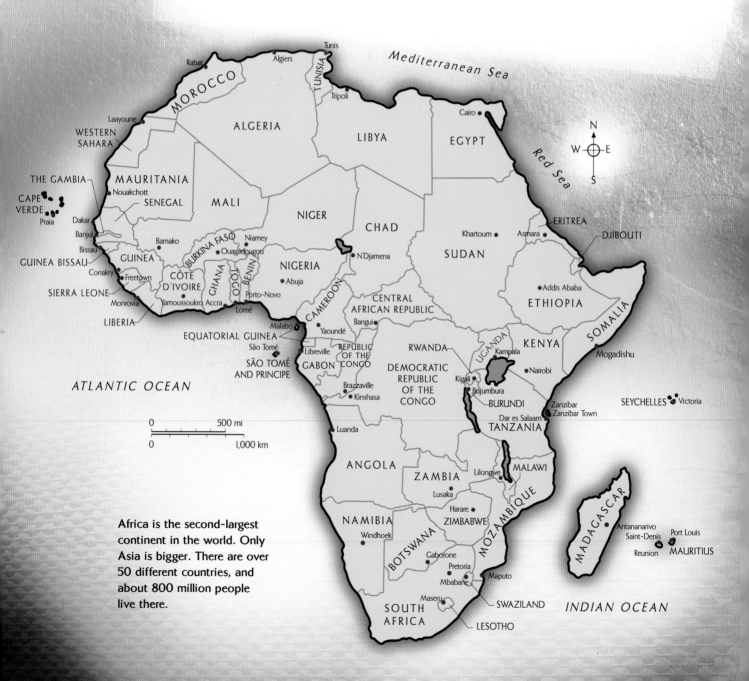

Africa is the second-largest continent in the world. Only Asia is bigger. There are over 50 different countries, and about 800 million people live there.

Full of variety

The land of Africa is full of variety. There are hot, dry deserts and warm, wet rainforests. In eastern Africa there are three of the world's biggest lakes. There are also large swamps and huge areas of grassland. The biggest mountain ranges are in eastern and southern Africa.

About 800 million people live in Africa. They speak more than 1,000 different languages.

Africa also has a huge variety of wildlife. Camels and scorpions live in the desert. Thousands of insects and many different monkeys live in the rainforest. The grassland is full of large mammals such as elephants, lions, leopards, zebras, and antelope.

African music is as varied as the continent. *Soukous* is infectious dance music from Congo. *Ga* drumming is traditional music from the villages of Ghana. *Taarab* is lush orchestral music from Tanzania, Kenya, and the island of Zanzibar. Zulu **a capella** is sweet harmony singing from South Africa.

The Mahotella Queens are a South African group. They have been making hit records in a Zulu style of music called *Mbaqanga* ("African jazz") since 1964.

The first people

Africa is thought to be the birthplace of the human race. Modern humans first lived in Africa about 150,000 years ago. In around 4000 BCE the first powerful **empires** appeared along the River Nile. The ancient Egyptian Empire is the best known of these. But we know little about the music of this time.

In early Africa there were probably about 10,000 different "nations". Some groups lived mostly by hunting animals and gathering plant foods. Some had herds of grazing animals and moved from place to place. Other groups were more settled.

The musical instruments that people used fitted their lifestyle and where they lived. Hunters, for instance, often used some kind of bow as an instrument. Forest people used wooden drums, because there was plenty of wood available.

Ancient tunes

Until recently African music was not written down. Songs and tunes were passed on from older musicians to younger ones by word of mouth. Some traditional African music may be very old, but because it was not written down, it is hard to know just how old a particular piece is.

These musicians are performing at a music festival in Algeria. The two musicians at the front are playing a kind of flute called a *nay* or *ney*. It is a classical Arab wind instrument.

The Soweto **Gospel** Choir was formed in South Africa in 2003. They have won many prizes, and in 2007 they were nominated (put forward) for an American Grammy award.

Trading with Arabia

Some time before 100 CE, African nations began trading abroad. On the east coast of Africa, Arab traders came for gold and **ivory**. In West Africa, a series of trading empires carried gold and salt across the Sahara Desert to Egypt and Arabia. They also traded in slaves. North Africans had strong links with the **Middle East**. Middle Eastern traders brought the **Muslim** religion to Africa.

Africans made musical connections with Arab people as well as trading with them. The music of North and East Africa was strongly influenced by Arabic music. West Africans also began to use Middle Eastern instruments, though they largely kept their own music.

Colonial Africa

In the 15th century European ships began trading along the West African coast. From the 16th to the 18th century, the main trade was in slaves. Millions of slaves were transported from Africa to North and South America.

The Africans who were taken to the Americas as slaves took their music with them. Over time this music changed, as people combined African sounds and rhythms with music from their new countries. In the 20th century, the combination of African and American music produced a rich variety of new musical styles. In North America musical styles such as the blues and jazz developed. In South America music such as Brazilian **samba** and Argentinean tango also had African connections.

In the 19th century, Europeans began to settle in Africa. They fought with each other and with local Africans to gain control of the land. By the late 19th century nearly all of Africa had been divided into **colonies**.

European rulers thought that African-style drumming was uncivilized. Instead, slaves were taught to sing hymns and play European dance music. African musicians began using European instruments, especially guitars. However, they continued to play and develop African-style music in private.

Jazz musician Duke Ellington (seated at the piano) wrote music that told the story of African slaves in the United States.

Today CDs of African music are popular throughout Africa, the United States, and Europe. This CD is a compilation from Putumayo Records, and features artists such as Afia Mala and Sam Mangwana.

Independence

From the 1950s African countries began to break free from their European rulers. However, independence did not solve Africa's problems. Most countries were left very poor. In some places, **dictators** took power and ruled by force. Wars broke out between some countries, or between groups within a country. African music has been affected by these wars and conflicts. Musicians have been put in jail or even killed for singing songs that were critical of their government.

African instruments

African instruments are as varied as the music they produce. There is an incredible range of instruments in Africa. In addition to traditional African instruments, most areas have adopted European instruments, and many areas also use **Middle Eastern** instruments.

Singing

The simplest instrument is the human voice, and singing is an essential part of nearly all African music. African songs can be about any subject. One kind of song that is found in many areas is the praise song. This is a song in which the singer praises an important person, or their ancestors. Praise singers also sing epic (long) songs about great events in the history of the people.

Busi Mhlongo (right), a South African singer and songwriter. She was the first female to record a *Maskanda* album. *Maskanda* is a type of Zulu **folk music**.

Call and response

One kind of singing that is very common in Africa is known as "call and response". This is when one singer sings a line or a verse of a song, and then another singer or a chorus responds to this line. The response can just be a repeat, or it can be a reply to the first line. In some songs one singer "calls" a line, and another improvises a smart reply. African slaves brought this style to the Americas, where call and response became a key part of **soul** and **gospel** music.

Wind instruments

Wind instruments are less common in traditional African music than other kinds of instrument. The main kinds of wind instruments are flutes and horns.

Some kinds of flute produce only one note. They are usually played in groups. Each player must play their particular note at the right moment, to produce a tune.

In North and East Africa, some musicians play wind instruments with one or two flat reeds in the mouthpiece. These instruments are similar to clarinets and oboes but they sound more like bagpipes.

Reed instruments like this are common in Arabic music. An *arghul* (single-reed instrument) and a *mizmar* (double-reed instrument) are most commonly played in Egypt, at weddings or as an accompaniment for belly dancers.

From the 17th to 20th centuries, when Europeans ruled much of Africa, many Africans learned to play brass instruments, such as trumpets and saxophones. More modern kinds of African music often use these instruments.

Regis Gizavo is an accordion player from Madagascar, a southern African island. The accordion is a wind instrument, which consists of reeds, bellows, and a keyboard.

Many drums

Drums are probably the most important instruments in African music. Drums playing interlocking **rhythms** are at the heart of much African music. There are many different kinds of drum, and they can be made of many materials. Some drums have one skin, while others have a skin on each end.

Groups of drums are often designed to be played together. In parts of Uganda and Kenya, for instance, drum groups play sets of five, seven, or fifteen drums, each drum tuned to a different note.

A West African hourglass drummer can play a range of different notes on a single drum. The hourglass drum is double-headed, and it narrows in the centre. The two drum skins are connected by many strings. The drummer holds the drum under his arm. By squeezing the strings with his arm they can make the drum skin tighter, and get a higher note. Squeezing less tightly slackens off the skin and gives a lower note.

Pitch messages

In some African languages, each word or part of a word has a particular **pitch**. In these languages, drum notes of different pitches can sound similar to words. In the past, slit drums with a number of different notes were used for long-distance communication. The different pitches of the drum could be played in different ways to produce messages.

Hourglass drums are found mainly in West Africa. Normally the player tucks the drum under his arm as he plays. By squeezing the strings along the sides of the drum, he can tighten the drum skin and produce a higher sound.

Shakers and pluckers

After the drum, the most common kinds of African instruments are ones that are shaken or hit. Shakers are metal discs strung on a wire, or beads wrapped round a gourd (a large hard-skinned fruit that has been hollowed out).

Gongs, finger bells, slit "drums" (made from a hollow piece of wood with a slit in it), and cowbells (iron bells without a clapper) are all designed to be hit in some way. *Balafons* (xylophones) are common in many parts of Africa.

The thumb piano is one of Africa's most characteristic instruments. It has a series of thin metal strips fastened at one end. Each strip makes a particular note when it is plucked. In Zimbabwe thumb pianos have been played for over 1,000 years, and can even be heard today in pop music. Three or more are often played together in a group, along with shakers and a hand drum.

Thumb pianos like this one are found across Africa. They are thought to have come originally from Zimbabwe, in southern Africa. Each metal key produces a different note when it is plucked.

From bows to lute harps

Many different kinds of string instruments also come from Africa. Perhaps the simplest of these is the mouth bow. This is a single-stringed instrument like the bow from a bow and arrow. The mouth bow is one of the oldest instruments in the world.

Players hold their mouth close to the string, and hit the string on a spot along its length. They change the shape of their mouth to get different sounds. A clear, but quiet, melody is produced.

The string of the mouth bow can be made from horsehair, sinew (a material in the body that holds together muscle and bone), or wire. The curved piece that you can see in the photograph below is made from wood or bone.

The mouth bow is usually played on its own, as a solo instrument. This boy is playing his mouth bow in Botswana, southern Africa.

There are many other African stringed instruments, including the one-string fiddle (violin), which is played with a bow. There are also two-stringed or four-stringed versions.

Many stringed instruments are used by solo singers to accompany themselves as they sing. The *ngoni* or *xalam* (a type of **lute** that has up to five strings) is used in this way. The 21-stringed West African **kora** is also often played by itself.

In many kinds of African music, guitars are used instead of lutes or other traditional stringed instruments. In Madagascar, for instance, there are many superb guitarists. Guitars were first brought to Madagascar from Asia, by Arab traders.

Malian musician Toumani Diabaté plays a stringed instrument called a *kora*. The strings stretch forwards from the tall pole and attach to the large gourd at the bottom.

Toumani Diabaté

Toumani Diabaté was born in 1965, and is a *kora* player from Mali in West Africa. He comes from a family of **griots**, or royal musicians, who in the past played for the king or chief. His father, Sidiki Diabaté, was also a great *kora* player. He first played outside Mali at the age of 19, when he performed with the Malian singer Kandia Kouyate. Two years later he recorded his first *kora* CD, which was very successful. Toumani has played with flamenco guitarists, jazz trombonists, blues singers, and many other musicians from other countries.

Putting on the style

Different regions in Africa have different musical styles. The biggest differences are between North Africa, where the music is Arabic (**Middle Eastern**) in style, and the rest of the continent. However, African music is not easily divided into compartments. Some music from North Africa sounds like music from farther south. Also, some West African and East African music has an Arabic sound.

Cesaria Evora

Cesaria Evora was born in 1941. She comes from Cape Verde, a small group of islands off West Africa. She sings the *morna*, a melancholy singing style that is popular in Cape Verde. Until she was 44, Cesaria only sang in Cape Verde. Then in 1985 she was chosen to represent Cape Verde at a music festival in Portugal. The concert was a great success and within a few years she had released an album that sold around the world.

Cesaria Evora is a singer from the Cape Verde islands. She is often called the Barefoot Diva (a diva is a very good singer) because she usually sings barefoot.

Gnawa is a kind of religious music from North Africa. *Gnawa* ceremonies often go on all night. They involve acrobatic dancing as well as music.

North African music

The music of North Africa is mostly Moorish or Arabic. It differs from other African music in several ways. The **scales** in Arabic music sound different. The intervals (gaps) between the notes can be much smaller than in other African music. The singing is also different. The singer adds many small **trills** and **slides** to the tune. The music often includes stringed instruments such as the *rebec* (fiddle) and the *oud* (**lute**). There are also reed instruments similar to clarinets and oboes.

Morocco is the centre of music in North Africa. The majority of people in Morocco are Berbers. Berbers are the original desert people of this area.

One kind of traditional Berber music is sung by poets, accompanied by drums and a chorus. The lead singer improvises (makes up) the words to the songs, which are sung back to him by the chorus.

Moroccans also play and listen to a kind of traditional Arab music known as *andalous*. This is a type of Moroccan **"classical" music** played by professionals. *Andalous* music came from Spain during the time it was a **Muslim** country (from around 714 CE until the mid-13th century). It is played by an orchestra that includes fiddles, lutes, and drums.

West and central African music

In West Africa traditional groups from the Ga and Dagomba people of Ghana are made up mostly of drummers and singers. However, there are other musical styles, too. At celebrations, the Fula people of Ghana play flutes, drums, and shakers, as well as sing. In northern Ghana and Burkina Faso, *balafon* (xylophone) music is important. Forest people play a range of wooden *balafons*, including giant ones each played by two people.

In Mali, Senegal, and Gambia, string instruments and singing are at the centre of musical life. One of the oldest kinds of surviving music in Africa was originally played by groups of hunters on six-stringed harps. *Mande* "classical" music is related to this hunters' music. It was originally played at royal courts by **griots**.

These musicians are from the Bobo tribe, in Burkina Faso. The *balafon* (below left) is a huge instrument. It is usually played by two people, but here it has just one player.

Central Africa

Much of central Africa is rainforest. There are many different kinds of traditional music from this area. Many of them involve the *likembe* (the local name for the thumb piano), xylophones, and drums.

The people who have lived longest in the rainforest are tribes such as the Baka, Mbuti, and Efé. These people are often known as Pygmies. Pygmy people have a rich, complex vocal music that is unlike other types of music in the area. They use sounds and music to communicate in the forest, and to make it more enjoyable to do jobs around the home camp.

Griot music

Mali was the centre of a great **empire** in the 13th century. The empire was founded in 1235 by the emperor Sunjata Keita. Since that time, Mali royal musicians, or *griots*, have played music for the rulers and powerful chiefs. Traditional *griot* music tells the history of the country. The songs are stories of kings, battles, love, and magic.

A young Baka musician plays the *ieta*. This seven-stringed instrument is a simple version of the West African *kora*. The *ieta* is not a traditional Baka instrument, and so musicians have only started playing it in the last 30 years or so.

East and southern African music

The music of East Africa is probably more varied than that of any other region. Along the coast, Taarab music is a mix of African, Arab, and Indian sounds. Inland, there is a huge range of different musical sounds.

Among Kenyan cattle-herding people such as the Maasai, the Samburu, and the Fulani, singing is the main form of music. The Akamba people of Kenya are great drummers and athletic dancers. In Uganda there are xylophone groups and trumpet bands, while Burundi is famous for the Royal Drummers, who play large, very powerful wooden drums. These drums can now be heard in pop music from Burundi.

The home of Taarab music is the island of Zanzibar, just off the coast of Tanzania. Traditional Taarab music is played by orchestras like this one.

These traditionally dressed Zulu warriors are performing a dance at a Shembe celebration in KwaZulu Natal, South Africa. Shembe takes place each year, and runs for the entire month of October.

Southern Africa

The San, or Bushmen, were the first people to live in southern Africa. The music of the San people today involves singing to drums, flutes, and musical bows.

Singing is important in music across southern Africa. The Zulu, Xhosa, and Sotho people arrived from farther north during the 17th century, and brought their style of singing with them. Singers sing two or three musical phrases, not at the same time but overlapping with each other. This creates an interweaving mix of voices.

In Zimbabwe, *mbira* (thumb piano) music is another strong tradition. *Mbira* music first began in Zimbabwe, and there are still many groups playing it today.

Angolan music has strong links to the music of Brazil. Both countries were ruled by Portugal at some time in their history, and many Angolans were sold as slaves to work in sugar and coffee plantations in Brazil. The lively **rhythms** of Angolan *semba* music are the basis of Brazilian **samba**.

Rhythm and song

When people outside Africa think of African music, they usually think of drums. We have seen that there is much more to African music than drums. However, drums are important. This is because **rhythm** is at the heart of African music. Drums often give African music its rhythm.

Like the Burundi Royal Drummers, these drummers from Rwanda play interlocking rhythms on a set of large, powerful drums.

Music scales

Most western music is based on a **scale** that has seven steps between the first note and the last (the **octave**). Different styles of African music use different scales. These can have four, five, six, or seven steps between the first note and the last. Some African scales have notes that are not found in western music.

Different rhythms

In western music, the rhythm is often a single strand of the sound, with everyone feeling the same beat. It might be a waltz-type rhythm (1–2–3, 1–2–3), a marching rhythm (1–2, 1–2), or a 4-beat rhythm. It could be a regular beat or a more irregular, skipping kind of rhythm.

In African music, the rhythm often works in a different way. Several musicians will be playing different rhythms at the same time. You can sometimes hear this clearly at the start of the music, when the drummers and other rhythm players start playing one by one. Music in which there are several rhythms playing at once is called **polyrhythmic** music. Sometimes the different rhythms do not seem to match, but together they make a complex and interesting sound.

Singing in rounds

The point at which a player begins playing has an effect on the overall rhythm that is produced. Sometimes two or more players play the same rhythm, but they begin it at different times. The result is like a "round", a song where people sing the same tune but begin singing at different times. You may have sung a simple round such as "Frère Jacques" or "Row, Row, Row Your Boat".

Keeping in time

It is not only drummers who are involved in forming the rhythms in a piece of African music. Different instruments can play in a rhythmic way that ties in with the drums, shakers, and other percussion instruments. Singing is also part of the mix.

In African group music, there are often several drummers and other instruments all following different rhythms, and perhaps playing at different times. It can sometimes be hard for musicians to hear their place in this music.

In order to keep everyone together, many pieces have a "timeline pattern". This is a simple, short pattern played again and again on an instrument such as a cowbell, which can be heard clearly above the other instruments. If a player stops and then comes in again, or if they cannot hear some of the other parts clearly, they can listen to the timeline pattern and hear how their own part should fit into the mix.

These men from Benin, western Africa, are playing drums alongside a cowbell (see seated man behind the drum, in the white vest), which keeps them all in time.

Even a musician playing alone can play polyrhythmic music. They can do this by playing one rhythm with the left hand and another rhythm with the right. Drummers, **kora** players, *mbira* players, and many other African solo musicians do this.

A soloist can also wear ankle bells and beat a rhythm with these, or tap on the side of their instrument to make rhythmic noises. Unless they are playing a wind instrument, they will also probably sing, and the phrasing of the song can add another layer of rhythm to the music.

The Kenyan musician Ayub Ogada plays an instrument called the *Luo lyre*. He also sings and adds extra rhythms with bells on his ankles.

Singing

Singing is another important part of African music. We have seen that among groups such as the Pygmy people, the Maasai, and Zulus, the music is mostly vocal (sung). In group singing, there are two main singing styles. In the first, everyone sings in the same rhythm and at the same time, but the different parts are higher or lower-**pitched**. The singers are singing the same music in harmony with each other. This kind of singing is often found in "call and response" music. A lead singer sings a line by themselves, then a chorus of several people sing a response, together and in harmony with each other.

In the second kind of group singing, the individual parts within the whole are different from each other, and the singers do not start or end at the same time. The different vocal parts overlap to make new notes and rhythmic patterns, in the same way that the rhythm parts in African music overlap with each other.

Fat and thin

In many African languages, different notes are not described as being "high" or "low". High notes are "small" or "thin", and low notes are "big" or "fat".

Singing is an important part of religion in Africa. These singers from the Democratic Republic of the Congo sing together in a **Christian** choir.

Blues singer Joe Turner was known as a blues "shouter". The gruff singing style he used may have originally come from African music.

Buzzes, rasps, and jingles

In western **classical music**, musicians aim to produce pure, clear notes from their instruments. African music is very different.

Drums often have metal jingles that rattle as the drum is played, while string instruments are often made so that the strings make a buzzing noise as they are played. Thumb pianos also have attachments that rattle or buzz.

Africans often sing in a clear, open voice, but in some music styles the singers use a rasping tone, or whisper. Singers **slide** between notes, and add "decorations" to the tune. Songs also often include shouts, whistles, and chanting.

Since the 20th century, African ideas about how voices and instruments can sound have affected music in the West. **Blues** singers, for instance, often have a rough, rasping voice and slide between notes, while some jazz saxophonists make the notes buzz or hiss as they play.

Everyday music

African music is not something separate from everyday life. Music-making is part of most social occasions. Traditional African music includes cradle songs, work songs, wedding music, and funeral music. African music is also part of religious rituals and entertainment for royalty. A woman with a crying baby might sing a cradle song to try and quiet it.

A cradle song

This is an example of a cradle song from Ghana, in western Africa. An older sister, grandmother, or neighbour might sing this to a child.

Where has your mother gone?

She has gone to fetch firewood.

What did she leave for you?

She left some bananas.

May I have one?

No! I won't give you any.

Are you crying? You mustn't.

Are you singing? You mustn't.

These Nigerian children are singing and clapping together in their school playground.

Music while you work

When Baka Pygmies go hunting in the rainforest, the hunt is begun with the women singing a *yelli*. This is a series of **yodelling** cries, beginning slowly and building to a climax. The hunters say that performing the *yelli* makes the animals easier to catch.

The *yelli* is an example of music while you work. Africans often sing or play music to make work more enjoyable. Groups of people grinding cereals into flour or putting a new floor in a house may sing a song as they work.

Work songs are usually informal music that is repeated many times. Many work songs are "call and response" songs, with one person singing the first line of the song and everyone else replying.

Music for special occasions

There are many special occasions in a person's life. A child is born, it becomes an adult, gets married, has children, and eventually dies. In Africa many of these stages in life involve special celebrations. A celebration can involve all kinds of features: a procession, speeches, dancing, masks, stories, and of course, music.

One celebration that is important in many parts of Africa is coming of age. This is the time when a boy becomes a man, or a girl becomes a woman. In parts of Ghana, girls who are coming of age spend several weeks learning about marriage and childcare from the adult women. At the end of this training period, the girls go round the town playing music, dancing, and collecting gifts of money.

Funeral ceremonies often involve music. There are also ceremonies to remember people after their death. The Sambaa people of Tanzania, for instance, hold a ceremony several years after a male relative has died.

These women from northern Kenya are singing and dancing to celebrate a wedding.

At many social events, the singers and musicians are not professionals. However, many African societies do have groups of professional musicians. The **griots** of Mali are one such group. In the past, *griots* played at the courts of emperors and other powerful rulers. Today's *griots* usually make their money from concerts and recordings. *Griots* know a large number of old songs, and make up many new ones. Many of them are praise songs, in which the *griot* sings about the greatness of the ruler and their ancestors.

For special occasions, men of the Karo tribe in Ethiopia paint their faces and bodies.

Ali Farka Touré

Ali Farka Touré (1939–2006) grew up in Niafunké, a small town in northern Mali. He first became interested in music at traditional African religious ceremonies. He learned the *njarka* (one-stringed fiddle) and the *ngoni* (five-stringed harp), but then took up the guitar. His music had strong connections with the American blues. In 1994 Touré won a U.S. Grammy award for his album *Talking Timbuktu*, made with U.S. guitarist Ry Cooder. However, he remained in Niafunké and spent his money on improving his farm. In 2004 Touré became mayor of Niafunké. In 2005 he won a second Grammy for his record *In the Heart of the Moon*, made with *kora* player Toumani Diabaté.

Religious music

About 45 percent of Africans are **Christians**, and about 50 percent are **Muslims**. The rest follow traditional African religions.

Europeans brought church music to Africa along with Christianity. Today most church music in Africa is **gospel** music, similar to Afro-American gospel.

For most Muslims singing and dancing are not religious activities. However, one group of Muslims, known as Sufis, use song and dance as part of their religious ceremonies. There are Sufi groups in Morocco and other parts of North Africa. In their ceremonies, Sufis sing the name of Allah (God) over and over again while they spin and dance. They believe that these dances bring them closer to Allah.

Another kind of Muslim music, known as *gnawa*, is also found in Morocco. *Gnawa* music has a more African sound than Sufi music.

Music and dancing are important parts of most traditional African religious ceremonies. People believe that during these ceremonies, a spirit may enter their body. Each person has one particular spirit who comes to them. The musicians play different music for different spirits.

In South Africa, gospel choirs sing at every important public occasion.

Country connections

There are strong connections between some African religions and religions in South America and the Caribbean. *Candomblé*, for example, is a Brazilian religion that is similar to a kind of worship found among the Yoruba people of Nigeria in the 18th and 19th centuries. The religious music is similar, too.

Years ago, Maasai boys had to kill a lion before they were true warriors. Today hunting lions is illegal, but young warriors still compete to see who can jump highest.

Warrior music

In the past, war was often part of life for men, and there were many songs and dances related to going to war. Only a few such warrior songs are still sung.

Among the Maasai people of Kenya, boys become *morani*, or warriors, when they are 15 years old. The *morani* live outside the village and perform special songs and dances together. In the songs each *moran* boasts about his skill at hunting, and in the dancing he tries to jump higher than all the others.

Modern African music

African popular music is mainly music of the cities. During the second half of the 20th century, many African people moved from villages to large towns and cities. In the city people do not have such strong links to the traditional music of the past.

African jazz

From the 1920s onwards, African musicians began listening to jazz. Jazz music has strong African connections. It was developed in the United States in the early 20th century by African Americans, the descendants of former slaves. Many African musicians learned to play the trumpet or saxophone, and listened to jazz music on the radio and on records.

Jazz styles first became popular in southern Africa. In the 1940s bands combined **swing music** with an African style called *marabi*. The result was called "African jazz", or *mbaqanga*. In the 1950s a number of singers became famous singing African jazz. The most successful was Miriam Makeba. Songs such as "The Click Song" and "Patha Patha" were hits in the United States in the 1960s. Today she is still one of the best known African singers outside her own country.

Miriam Makeba became known around the world. She even performed at President Kennedy's birthday party in 1959. Here she performs in Helsinki, Finland, in 1969.

African dance music

In the 1920s Ghana was still a British **colony** called the Gold Coast. In the high-class clubs and hotels, bands of African musicians played American music for visitors. However, late in the evening they played music that mixed jazz with West African styles. It became known as "highlife".

In the 1960s highlife bands went electric. Finger-picking electric guitar became the main sound. During the 1970s Ghana's **economy** collapsed and there was little work for highlife musicians. Many moved to Nigeria or to Britain. However, by the 1990s a new type of highlife was popular in Ghana. This was "hiplife", a mixture of highlife and rap music.

In the early 1970s Sam Mangwana sang with the best *soukous* bands in the Congo. Then in 1976 he left to tour other parts of Africa. He was one of the first musicians to spread interest in *soukous* music.

Soukous

Soukous was another kind of dance music developed in the Congo. It was based on **rumba**, a kind of dance music from Cuba. In the 1950s there were hundreds of soukous bands across Africa. By the 1960s the guitarists were playing electric guitars, and trumpets and saxophones had become part of the sound.

Protest music

While they were being ruled by Europeans, Africans fought for independence (freedom to rule themselves). However, after independence some African countries were taken over by **dictators** who ruled the country by force. Musicians often became involved in the struggle for freedom from unfair rulers.

In the 1970s, black people in Rhodesia (now Zimbabwe) began a rebellion against the government, which was made up only of whites. The word for rebellion in the Shona language is *chimurenga*. As part of the rebellion, **pirate radio** stations broadcast *chimurenga* music (songs supporting the rebellion). Many musicians who wrote *chimurenga* songs, such as Thomas Mapfumo, were arrested and put in prison.

Musicians criticizing their government in other countries also got into trouble. In 1963 Miriam Makeba spoke out against apartheid at a meeting of the **United Nations** in the United States. As a result she was not allowed to return to South Africa until 1990.

Apartheid

Apartheid means "separateness". It was the name of a set of laws passed in South Africa in 1948. At the time South Africa was an independent country ruled by an all-white government. Apartheid laws separated black and coloured (mixed race) people from the whites. Black people were allowed to live only in certain places, they were not allowed to do many types of job, and they had to have special passes to travel from place to place. For years black South Africans protested against the unfair laws. However, apartheid did not end until the 1990s.

Oumou Sangare

Oumou Sangare was born in Bamako (the Malian capital) in 1968, but her parents were from the Wassulu region in the south of Mali. She is the greatest singer in the Wassulu style of southern Mali. It is accepted in Mali that a man can have many wives. Through her music Oumou Sangare campaigns against this tradition, and against arranged marriages where women are married against their will.

In the 1970s, Nigerian singer Fela Kuti invented a new style of music called Afro-Beat. It was a combination of highlife with American jazz and funk. In his songs, Fela Kuti was very critical of the Nigerian government. In 1984 he was jailed for five years because of his outspoken views.

World music success

Improved communications brought many changes to music in Africa. Radio, TV, records, cassettes, CDs, and the Internet have made it possible for people to listen to all kinds of music. Rock, pop, Latin, and other music from the United States are all now accessible. Hearing this kind of music has changed the way Africans make their own music. Some African musicians have become international stars, who play packed-out concerts and sell millions of copies of their albums. Most of the big African music stars are from southern or West Africa.

In the 1980s, Europeans and Americans began to listen to "World Music" (music from other cultures). *Soukous* was one of the most popular World Music styles, especially in France and England. In the late 1980s many *soukous* musicians moved to Europe. By the 1990s people were playing *soukous*-based music in Paris and London as well as in Congo.

African music, such as these Egyptian CDs, is now popular throughout the world.

Franco Luambo Makiadi

Franco Luambo Makiadi (above) was born in 1938 and grew up in Kinshasa, in what was then called Zaire (now the Democratic Republic of the Congo). When he was very young he made himself a tin-can guitar, with electrical wire for strings. At the age of 11 he got his first real guitar, and by 15 he was a guitar wizard playing in several Kinshasa bands. At the age of 18 he set up his own band, OK Jazz, which was soon popular outside Congo. In the 1960s he recorded in Europe, and he became known as the "sorcerer of the guitar". When he died in 1989, there were four days of mourning in Zaire.

African stars

South African singer Miriam Makeba and trumpeter Hugh Masekela were among the first Africans to be successful abroad. Nigerian musician King Sunny Ade made an album called *Juju Music* in 1982, which was one of the first successful World Music albums. He was followed by other stars such as Salif Keita and Mory Kanté from Mali, Youssou N'Dour and Baba Maal from Senegal, and *rai* singer Khaled.

The Algerian singer Khaled is king of the musical style known as *rai*. In 2002 Khaled was the first Arabic musician to tour in the United States after the September 11 terrorist attacks.

One way that African musicians have become more popular abroad has been by teaming up with western musicians. Youssou N'Dour has had chart hits in Britain and the United States in duets with Peter Gabriel, Neneh Cherry, and Dido. Ladysmith Black Mambazo became internationally famous after singing on Paul Simon's record *Graceland*. Damon Albarn of the band Gorillaz made an album with several Malian musicians, including **kora** player Toumani Diabaté.

Senegalese singer Youssou N'Dour is one of the biggest stars of World Music. In 2005 he sang his hit song "7 seconds" with British singer Dido at the UK Live 8 concert.

Youssou N'Dour

The music of Senegalese singing star Youssou N'Dour (born 1959) is called *mbalax*. It developed in Senegal during the 1970s. *Mbalax* is a good example of the mix of African and western elements in popular music. The style is based on traditional drum music found in many parts of West Africa. However, some drum parts are played by modern western instruments such as electric guitars and keyboards. In 2005 Youssou N'Dour won a Grammy award for Best Contemporary World Music album.

Growing and changing

African popular music continues to grow and change all the time. In the past, African musicians played thumb pianos, single-string fiddles, and hourglass drums. Today they often play electric guitars and keyboards, or make all-electronic dance tracks. Many younger musicians are playing African versions of modern American music such as **house**, **trance**, and **hip hop**.

Kwaito is a popular South African music style that began as a version of American house music but has become more African in style. Nigerian rappers such as JJC and the 419 Squad are beginning to win an international following. Hip hop artists in Senegal are producing music that adds new ideas and sounds to hip hop rather than just copying American styles.

In modern Africa, especially in the cities, the place of music in people's lives has changed. Making and dancing to music is less a part of everyday life. Musicians play concerts and dances, and record cassettes and CDs. Fans listen to the music at home, or go to concerts to hear their favourites.

Some people worry that "real" African music is being lost as African musicians copy non-African styles. However, music in Africa remains as varied as in the past, perhaps more so. Many kinds of traditional music have continued to the present day, and some that were dying out have been revived. Traditional music is at the root of most popular music. However, young musicians are also introducing new instruments, new ideas, and new styles into the mix. African music has a bright future.

This photograph shows one of the most successful African rap groups, Daara J. They are from Senegal, and have been playing their own brand of rap music since 1997.

A world of music

	String Instruments	Brass Instruments	Wind Instruments
Africa	*oud* (**lute**), *rebec* (fiddle), **kora** (harp-lute), *ngoni* (harp), musical bow, one-string fiddle	*kakaki* or *wazi* (metal trumpets), horns made from animal horns	*naga, nay sodina* (flutes), *arghul, gaita* (single-reed instruments), *mizmar* (double-reed instrument)
Australia, Hawaii, and the Pacific	ukulele (modern), guitar (modern)		flutes, nose flutes, didgeridoo, conch shell horns
Eastern Asia	*erhu* (fiddle), *dan tranh, qin, koto, gayageum* (derived from *zithers*)	gongs, metallophones, xylophones	*shakuhachi* (flute), *khaen* (mouth organ), *sralai* (reed instrument)
Europe	violin, viola, cello, double bass, mandolin, guitar, lute *zither*, hurdy gurdy (**folk** instruments)	trumpet, French horn, trombone, tuba	flute, recorder, oboe, clarinet, bassoon, bass clarinet, saxophone, accordion, bagpipes
Latin America and the Caribbean	*berimbau* (musical bow), *guitarrón* (bass guitar), *charango* (mandolin), *vilhuela* (high-**pitched** guitar)	trumpet, saxophone, trombone (salsa instruments)	*bandoneon* (button accordion)
Western Asia	*sitar, veena, oud, dombra, doutar, tar* (lutes) *rebab, kobyz* (fiddles) *sarod, santoor, sarangi*	trumpets	*bansuri, ney* (flutes), *pungi/been* (clarinets), *shehnai, sorna* (oboes)

Percussion Instruments	Vocal Styles	Dance Styles
balafon (wooden xylophone), *mbira* (thumb piano), bells, slit drums, friction drums, hourglass drums, conventional drums	open throat singing, Arabic style singing: this is more nasal (in the nose) and includes many **trills** and ornaments	spiritual dancing, mass dances, team/formation dances, small group and solo dances, modern social dances
drums, slit drums, rattles, clapsticks, gourds, rolled mats	*oli* (sung by one person), *mele* (poetry), hula, *himene* (choral music), Dreaming songs	hula, seated dances, *fa'ataupati* (clapping and singing), haka
taiko (drums)	*p'ansori* (single singer), *chooimsae* (verbal encouragement), folk songs	Peking/Beijing opera, Korean folk dance
side drum, snare drum, tambourine, *timpani* (kettle drums), cymbals, castanets, bodhran, piano	solo ballad, work song, hymn, plainchant, opera, Music Hall, cabaret, choral, homophony (harmony, parts moving together), polyphony (independent vocals together)	jig, reel, sword dance, clog dance, *mazurka* (folk dances), **flamenco**, country dance, waltz, polka, ballet, *pavane, galliard* (16th century)
friction drum, steel drums, bongos (small drums), congas (large drums), *timbales* (shallow drums), maracas (shakers), *guiro* (scraper)	toasting	*zouk* (pop music), tango, lambada, **samba**, *bossa nova* (city music), **rumba**, mambo, *merengue* (salsa)
tabla drum, *dhol* drum, tambourine, *bartal* cymbals, bells, sticks, gongs	bards, *bhangra* (Punjabi), *qawwali* (Sufi music), throat singing, *ghazals* (love poems)	*bhangra, dabke* (traditional dances), Indian classical, whirling dervishes, belly dancing

Glossary

a capella singing with no musical accompaniment

blues kind of African-American music that developed in the southern United States in the early 1900s

Christian someone who believes in Jesus Christ, the son of God

classical music traditional or long-established form of music

colony region or territory under the direct control of a distant country

dictator ruler with total power over a country

economy management of money, goods, and property in a country

empire large area or group of countries ruled by one leader or government

flamenco type of Spanish music played mainly on the guitar, with singing and dancing

folk music traditional music of a particular area

gospel soulful kind of music sung in praise of God

griot royal musician from West Africa

hip hop kind of American urban (city) music in which DJs rap (talk rhythmically) over music or another backing

house kind of electronic dance music that developed in the United States in the 1980s

ivory material that elephant tusks are made of

kora stringed instrument with a large gourd for a body, and a tall pole with many strings coming out of it. It is played upright, like a harp.

lute stringed instrument with an oval body and a bent neck, which is played like a guitar

marabi South African music from the 1920s–1930s. It combined African styles with American jazz.

Middle East countries in the area between Egypt in the west and Iran in the east

Muslim someone who believes in the religious teachings of the prophet Muhammad

octave interval between the first and eighth note of a scale. The eighth note has the same name as the first note, but is higher.

pirate radio radio station that broadcasts illegally (without permission from the government)

pitch how high or low a sound is

polyrhythmic music that involves several rhythms played at the same time

rai North African music that is popular in Algeria

reggae style of popular music from Jamaica

rhythm beat behind a piece of music

rumba African-style, Cuban dance music. Rumba is also a Latin-American ballroom dance style.

samba kind of loud drum music from Brazil

scale set of notes organized in regular upward or downward steps

slide note that slides smoothly from one pitch to another

sorcerer person who practises magic. It can also be used to describe someone who has a special talent.

soul American music that was invented in the 1950s. It combines jazz, blues, and gospel music.

swing music kind of jazz played by big bands

trance being unaware of your surroundings. Someone in a trance looks like they are asleep.

trill note that wobbles rapidly

United Nations international organization. It was set up after World War II to maintain peace and security across the world.

yodelling singing that shifts quickly from high to low notes

Further information

Books

The History of Gospel Music, Rose Blue and Corinne J. Naden (Chelsea House, 2001)

The Zulu of Africa, Nita Gleimius, Emma Mthimunye, and Evelina Sibanyoni (Lerner, 2003)

Websites

African Music Radio
http://www.africanmusicradio.com/amr/

Calabash Music
http://news.calabashmusic.com/world/getstarted

Music of the Baka Forest People
http://www.baka.co.uk/baka/bakamsc.htm

National Geographic World Music
http://worldmusic.nationalgeographic.com/
worldmusic/view/page.basic/home

Smithsonian Global Sound
http://www.smithsonianglobalsound.org/
index.aspx

The Story of Africa
http://www.bbc.co.uk/worldservice/africa/
features/storyofafrica/

Thumb piano tunes
http://pbskids.org/africa/piano/haveflash.html

Organizations

The Africa Centre in London:
http://www.africacentre.org.uk/whatson.htm
This is the main African cultural organization in Britain, but at the moment it is closed for redevelopment. However, the website does provide some information about African culture in Britain.

African Cultural Centre in Worcester:
http://www.african-museum.com/
This centre provides information about Africa, its traditions, cultures, art, and history, and its many contributions to the rest of the world

African music news for Australia:
http://www.africanoz.com.au/
This website gives details about African music and events going on throughout Australia.

Places to visit

A great place to visit for West African music is Aklowa in Bishop's Stortford:
http://www.aklowa.net/bmn/music/Aklowa.
nsf/Document?ReadForm&DocTitleWelcome%20
and%20News

This is an African cultural centre run by a Ghanaian musician called Felix Cobbson.

You could also go to an African music performance, or a dance workshop, in your area:
http://www.bbc.co.uk/africabeyond/

This BBC website has excellent listings of African music, dance, and other cultural events around the country.

Index

a capella 5
accordions 11
Ade, King Sunny 40
African continent 4, 5
African history 6–9
Afro-Beat 37
Algeria 6, 40
andalous music 17
Angola 21
ankle bells 25
apartheid 37
Arabic influences 6, 7, 16, 17, 20

bells 13, 24, 25
Benin 24
Berber music 17
blues 4, 27, 31
Botswana 14
brass instruments 11, 44
Burkina Faso 18
Burundi 20
buzzes and rasps 27

call and response songs 10, 26, 29
candomblé 33
Cape Verde 16
celebrations and social events 18, 21, 30–1
chimurenga music 36
click sounds 21
coming of age ceremonies 30
Congo 5, 26, 35
cowbells 13, 24
cradle songs 28, 29

Daara J 43
dancing 20, 21, 33, 43, 45
Diabaté, Toumani 15, 31, 41
drums and drumming 6, 8, 12, 18, 19, 20, 22, 23, 24, 25, 27, 41, 43
    ga drumming 5
    hourglass drums 12, 42
    slit drums 12, 13

Ellington, Duke 8
Ethiopia 31
Evora, Cesaria 16

fiddles 15, 17, 31, 42
finger bells 13
finger-picking 25, 35
flutes 6, 11, 18
funeral ceremonies 30

ga drumming 5
Gambia 18
Ghana 5, 18, 30, 35
Gizavo, Regia 11
gnawa music 17, 32
gongs 13
gospel music 7, 10, 32
griots 18, 19, 31
guitars 8, 15, 25, 31, 35, 39, 41, 42

harmony singing 5, 26
harps 18, 31
highlife music 35, 37
hip hop 4, 42
hiplife music 35
hourglass drums 12, 42
house music 42

ieta 19

jazz and African jazz 4, 5, 8, 27, 34, 35, 37

Kanté, Mory 40
Keita, Salif 40
Kenya 5, 12, 20, 30, 33
Khaled 40
kora 15, 25
Kuti, Fela 37
kwaito music 42

Ladysmith Black Mambazo 41
lutes 15, 17
lyres 25

Maal, Baba 40
Maasai 20, 26, 33
Madagascar 11, 15
Mahotella Queens 5
Makeba, Miriam 34, 36, 40
Makiadi, Franco Luambo 39
Mali 18, 19, 31, 36, 40
Mangwana, Sam 9, 35
Mapfumo, Thomas 36
Masekela, Hugh 40
mbalax music 41
mbira music 21, 25
Mhlongo, Busi 10
modern popular music 34–43
morna 16
Morocco 17, 32
mouth bows 14
musical instruments 10–15, 44–5
musical styles 16–21
Muslim music 32
Mwenda, Jean Bosco 25

N'Dour, Youssou 40, 41
Nigeria 29, 33, 37, 42
notes, musical 23, 26

Ogada, Ayub 25
oral tradition 6
orchestral music 5, 17, 20

percussion instruments 12–13, 24, 45
pitch 12, 26
polyrhythmic music 23, 25
praise songs 10, 31
protest music 9, 36–7
Pygmy people 19, 26, 29

rai music 40
rap 4, 35, 42, 43
reed instruments 11, 17
reggae 4

religious music 17, 32–3
rhythms 4, 12, 22, 23, 24, 25, 26
polyrhythmic music 23, 25
rumba 35
Rwanda 22

samba 8, 21
San music 21
Sangare, Oumou 36
saxophones 11, 27, 35
scales 17, 23
Senegal 18, 40, 41, 42, 43
shakers 13, 18, 24
singing 5, 10, 16, 17, 18, 19, 20, 21, 25, 26, 27, 29, 40, 41, 45
    call and response songs 10, 26, 29
    gospel music 7, 10, 32
    harmony singing 5, 26
    morna 16
    praise songs 10, 31
    protest songs 9, 36, 37
    rounds 23
    vocal styles 45
    warrior songs 33
    work songs 29
slaves 8, 10, 21, 34
slit drums 12, 13
soukous music 5, 35, 38
South Africa 5, 7, 10, 21, 32, 36, 42
Soweto Gospel Choir 7
stringed instruments 14–15, 17, 18, 27, 44
Sufi music 32

taarab music 5, 20
tango 8
Tanzania 5, 30
thumb pianos 13, 19, 21, 27, 42
timeline pattern 24
Touré, Ali Farka 31
trance music 42
trumpets 11, 20, 35
Turner, Joe 27

Uganda 12, 20

vocal styles 45

warrior music 33
western music 8, 38, 41
wind instruments 6, 11, 44
work songs 29
World Music 38, 40, 43

xylophones 13, 18, 19, 20

yodelling 29

Zaire 39
Zanzibar 5, 20
Zimbabwe 13, 21, 36
Zulu people 5, 21, 26